I0755983

FINISHING LINE PRESS
www.finishinglinepress.com

The Winged & the Horned

poems by

Tammy C. Greenwood

Finishing Line Press
Georgetown, Kentucky

The Winged & the Horned

ISBN 979-8-89990-464-6 First Edition

ACKNOWLEDGMENTS

Thank you to the editors of the following journals and anthologies for supporting my work by publishing these poems (or versions) where they first appeared:

Bellevue Literary Review: "Call and Response"
Door is a Jar Literary Magazine: "How the Black Hole Sings" & "Small as a Figure in a Hudson River School Painting"
Humana Obscura: "Freefall"
McNeese Review: "Burnished Ordinary"
New Ohio Review: "I Should Have Known"
Orange Blossom Review: "Sea Glass and Agate"
Pinch Journal: "The Winged & the Horned"
Poetry South: "Assemblage"
Rust & Moth: "A Clearing" & "Raining Bones"
SWWIM: "Soldier's Heart"
Whale Road Review: "Survival Season"
Wild Roof Journal: "Left to the Sun"
Women in a Golden State Anthology, Gunpowder Press: "Hostile Environment"

Publisher: Leah Huete de Maines
Editor: Christen Kincaid
Cover Art: *Cryptid Wolpertinger* by Megan Carr, @megansillustration (www.megancarrillustration.co.uk)
Author Photo: Cean Orrett of Cean One Photography; www.ceanone.com
Cover Design: Elizabeth Maines McCleavy

Order online: www.finishinglinepress.com
also available on amazon.com

Author inquiries and mail orders:
Finishing Line Press
PO Box 1626
Georgetown, Kentucky 40324
USA

Contents

To my children, born from the heart—
Jessica, Victoria, and Nicholas

The Infertile Rabbit

My rabbit den is empty. I'm meant to make babies but how does prey have time for that. The coyotes survey the land by day, the fox his foot soldier, horned owls on night watch. Bees are singing but I can't make out the tune. So, I stay in my lair taming circus beetles to perform with shadow puppets in moonbeams. The spider crosses his tightrope unafraid, and I write stories of when I could fly. Flying beyond shingled roofs and smokestacks to where the river meets the waterfall, surrendering into the arms of the ocean. I wonder what it feels like to surrender.

Assemblage

As.sem.blage | art that is made by assembling disparate elements - often everyday objects—scavenged by the artist

A sculpture of found objects   she was made
    from mud of the Gulf   sediments of stardust
        digging through shale layers
            for the place that had never been wounded.

Collaged with antlers, snakeskin, and cicada shells
    arms draped in rosary beads and malas
        singing to all the gods
            while mantled in manzanita.

Each cell of her honeycombed hair
    tangled with relics   envied by the bowerbird
        her blemished heart   wrapped in words unfolding
            into welcomed wings   planted among
                milkweed and dandelion seeds.

Muddied Waters Are Thicker Than Blood

Another video of animals adopting lost
offspring—A tortoise mothering
a hippo, gorilla to a kitten, a dog to an owl.
It didn't take long for the algorithm
to figure me out. On the day we met, your three
small children clung to you like kudzu
to the pine. And again, on our wedding day
as they joined us at the altar to receive their rings
too. My promise to love and cherish them til death
do us part. We'd hoped to add more to the brood,
but monthly fertility clinic failures, and the children worrying,
would we love our baby more, proved too much. We left it
to the gods. On nights they cried for their mother, I held them
until our sorrows slept. Our backs like bookends propped
against walls of grief. So much time wasted wishing
for things that weren't missing. Now, as adults they soothe
themselves. In their wanderlust, find new ways
to remedy the pain, search for logic behind longing,
thinking the naming will tame it. Time is full of forgetting—
grief full of too much time. I still taste moments laid thick
like milk-skin on the sweetest vat of cream, hope after
the hippo reunites with his kind in the water,
that he'll miss the land and return to find his tortoise.

Another Baby Shower

Some days I'm happy
to eat pastel petit-fours

between columns of cotton-
candy-colored balloons.

Smile at communal stories
of carrying, and latching,

midnight cravings. Nod as though
I understand their expressions

seeing their eyes looking
back at them. Some days I'm happy

the doctor finally said, *it's time.*
My belly distended with fibroids,

removed the womb we kept hoping
would make room

for something new, rid me
of monthly reminders of defeat.

My fingers checking every fruit
for ripeness as I watch new red leaves

unfold against the green.
Other days I wonder how

to name this feeling that's left
on its own. How the moon continues

to rise every night, knowing
all there'll ever be is darkness.

Small as a Figure in a Hudson River School Painting

When we moved across country
I hummed Natalie's lyrics,

Go West, paradise is there.
It had taken all day to get through Texas

with its miles of tornado friendly flatlands
yielding nothing but tumbleweeds.

I'd never driven through mountains
but saw the Capitan towering in the distance,

sentry to painted deserts folded between
cliffs of dried seas like unanswered questions.

My senses vying for attention,
I turn down the radio so I can see.

Horizons of pumpjacks replaced by saguaro cactus,
cicadas surrender to desert crickets, Sonoran toads.

I imagine graffitied trains heading east
carrying messages home.

Funny how longing works, lingering on.
Somewhere between Albuquerque and the Mohave

I hold a whiptail lizard in the palm of my hand.
I know what it is to feel so small,

small as a figure in a Hudson River School painting,
colors hanging overhead like banners of papel picado,

and the night sky with its half-moon,
like the black belly of a whale,

his sleepy half-closed eye,
questioning my existence.

Hostile Environment

August holds charred remains of last year's fire
under glass—a dome of stifled air reigning
    green saplings. Yoked in reverence and sorrow,
    they worship at the feet of blackened Eucalyptus,
        whispering, *not yet.*

The day of my miscarriage, the doctors called
my womb a *hostile environment.* Said it's an unlikely place
    for anything to grow, sustaining only fibroids
    like the dead bramble I continue to water,
        praying for proof of resurrections.

Years later, after my hysterectomy, I asked
if I could have it. I wanted to incinerate it myself,
    toss it on a ceremonial fire
    fit for Viking queens—or Salem witches,
        I wasn't sure which.

We hike the Pacific Crest Trail in search of *fire followers,*
dormant blooms of mariposa lily and wild heliotrope,
    unleashed by fire from strangling chaparral.
    Feeding on cinders, they rise like little phoenix,
        all the evidence we need for today.

On Days Like These

I have to remind myself
          why I love this world—
that mornings still smell like returning jasmine,

the mist wrapping itself through canyons
          like a convergence of souls.

When the astronauts return from blackness,
          they enter the atmosphere ablaze,
a falling resurrection.

Their first recollection, the ambrosial musk
          of marine air—brininess of birth.

As if the honeyed sun melted into the sea
          with the remnants of dusk.

Next was the heaviness of their bodies,
          their limbs suddenly filled
with every earthly grievance.

It's hard to believe the burden they bear
          will lighten with gravity now upon them,

or that it wasn't the weight of the world
          they first noticed, but rather how much
they had missed its sweetness.

Anatomy Lesson

We coax a broken mollusk towards a vacated
home, wonder at its telescoping neck,

tentacled eyes probing the unoccupied husk.
Kneeled on bent elbows among the trace

of garden snails, surrounded by damaged
and war-wounded, we imagine occupants in exile,

vacant shells abandoned. When we learn
they don't need us at all— exoskeletons

regrowing like fingernails, the empty ones,
an evening meal, we consider what they must think

of us presenting their dead like a warning.
Leaving us with our own need to be needed.

Freefall

I don't know what made the baby barn owl
jump from the owl box last summer.

The midday sun creeping over 110 degrees,
the mother left to find shade in nearby trees,

leaving two offspring to fend for themselves.
Half his body still covered in flightless feathers,

like a torn parachute, he hurled himself
from twelve feet above the ground.

I waited to see if the sibling would follow.
As temperatures grew, three ravens gathered

on the box, their shadows cloaking the exit.
Sometimes fear is warm and familiar,

you don't realize it's slowly cooking you.
The grounded owlet made his way under

the split-rail fencing, almost camouflaged
under dense manzanita. Today the owl box

sits in silence as I stand in safety at the foothills.
The day grows hotter as ravens circle overhead.

Survival Season

even when heat and Santa Ana
          winds trip fire-watch apps,

ground squirrels lay splayed
          on tiled stoops, orange firestick

with their pleading fingers
          reach upwards to a cloudless sky,

winds blow so hard
          as if trying to resuscitate

buckwheat and sage,
          i can still make out the slender

wild oat and its ripening gold,
          the last of the lavender,

its scent finding its way
          through the pause.

i must stop calling the raven
          and barn owl, *mine*.

stop nursing dried milkweed
          as if I'd just given birth,

professing my sorrows
          to songbirds. so on mornings

like these when all that's left
          are remnants of fledgling wings,

i won't wonder if they left
          behind a night full of worry,

only imagine bobcat and coyote
        consumed their flight,

escaped the impermanence
        of all that's still gleaming.

Raining Bones

Today I found a hip-joint
entangled in the chicken wire,
small bones like offerings on the feeder
where I leave peanuts and boiled eggs.
A whole foot, still warmed by fur,
left in the birdbath by the pair of ravens
I'd hoped to tame. Corvids are known
to bring trinkets to those who feed them,
recognize the faces of enemies and friends.
But what does he see in mine
that he leaves me only rabbit bones
scattered among succulents and stones?
Bones dropped from high in the sky,
broken over boulders to expose the marrow.
Last spring there was a third raven.
Cawing an incantation, they pounced
in unison, up and down on the fence,
an annunciation of their multiplying.
I ponder the hunt, think how much
goes on in the night while I sleep.
All the small deaths and triumphs, the raining
of bones with all our marrow laid bare.

A Clearing

This morning I watch a red-tailed hawk float
along high wires, hunting in the clearing below.
Diving against a backdrop of desert, a mob of
ravens skip across him like stones in a pond.

The day of my father's funeral, a red-tailed hawk
sat on the utility pole across from the cemetery
in the middle of town. Sitting in the southern
rain as grief devoured the sun, we imagined

it was him, once a great hunter, until
he became the hunted. How fiercely and
quickly cancer came and conquered, a faceless
coward, no glance, no signal, no war-horns.

Now I sit at each sunrise as the hawk
fights off his inescapable foes, talons flung
high, sounding his warning, I watch him
win over and over again.

Soldier's Heart

They call it broken heart syndrome,
spawned by intense trauma or sorrow,

once named, *soldier's heart*—
worn out from its fighting, its witnessing.

Today the news said, the earth's core,
a solid iron heart, is slowing its rotation,
an irregular heartbeat

measured in seismic waves.
I wore a heart monitor the year

heroin entered our home a second time.
Surrendering another child to rehab,

I drove to the crest
of the San Jacinto Mountains, blackened by fire,
where charred saplings made sense.

They say my heart is broken,
pausing among the pines

so I can breathe.
I know how the iron core feels,

trying to reverse time,
to when flowers and children grew cradled,
yet wild, wandering untouched,

sunlight their only intoxication.

Sea Glass & Agate

sit in a bowl next to the photo
that looks black and white.

Not yet a man, he skips rocks
at Little Girls Pointe on Lake Superior,

its vastness lost in atmospheric haze,
him wrapped in grey light.

A distant lighthouse pulsating through
the fog, a premonition from some

unknowable shore, before the nights
laced with heroin became interlocked

with days, turning years into decades,
dragging him under.

They say the great lake *never gives up her dead*,
yet scattered survivors escape to the shore,

smooth and unscathed as this polished sea glass
held tightly in the palm of my hand.

Call and Response

When owl fledglings fall from their nest,
I consider not inserting myself into their fate,
watch the siblings hobble from the heat
to the safety of buckwheat. The mother arrives
at dusk with short shrill chirps, they answer
with a bellowing screech as if they'll never be found.
She drops night-kills in the brush,
their call and response puncture darkness
like luminescent blooms against the black sky.
It's been months since our last exchange,
your face nearly unrecognizable on a video call.
Another urban mayday, you considering rehab,
me knowing there's only moments to say
the right thing before you go silent again, wishing
a simple lullaby could still calm you in the night.
The next morning a group of ravens
gather in the shade, earn their name—an *unkindness*,
a clawed foot remaining between them.
A lone owlet drags himself from dried yarrow,
one wing flapping, the other dangling by its side.
It took only minutes to toss the towel over its body,
place it in the dog crate in the airconditioned car.
I'm not sure if an owl is soothed by, *You Are My Sunshin*e,
but I sing it all the way to the rescue,
knowing this is all that I can save.

But Soon the Spoonbill

The nurse says we should go see the sunset,
that you could get lost in the everglades.

All I can think is how anyone pauses despair
in search of beauty. That I'm still angry

with the sun as it continues to rise, sustaining
only sorrows. Besides, I'd already decided

to hate Florida—blamed it for your overdose,
how it swallowed you up, sunk you in its bog.

The road to the hotel is flanked by waterways,
flared with yellow warning signs,

flood zones and gator crossings
against every shade of muted green.

Then from the shoreline, rising
like a just-created demigod—or Hermes himself,

the color of daybreak, crimson feathered tunic,
shoulders of golden epaulettes.

Have you ever seen a Roseate Spoonbill?
An *exquisite corpse*, torso layered like tulle peonies,

alabaster head glowing like a crowned saint.
A tourniquet to grief, his feathers ignite

as his wingspan shifts to catch the light,
turning translucent as newborn flesh.

His hibiscus gaze, an incantation, a reminder
the sun not only shines for me.

When Longing Leaves

Sunlight enters through the open door severing my shadow into a midnight paper doll. She steps away from me, reaches for clouds drifting by windows like scenes from moving trains, knowing they will make her disappear. Bees lay breathless, covering the sill. Twined fur feet hang from butcher hooks overhead, trophies still warm from a morning hunt. The rabbit watches from the doorway, she wears my orange dress. Her mortar and pestle rest, she serves me tea from the tree of intangibles. My shadow, now shed, slithers across planked floors, through panes of glass, vanishing beneath the clouded sky.

The Scales and the Scorpion

The new moon paints the sky black,
Milky Way, a white river, carries chariots
and gods. Perseids at their peak, we lie crown
to crown, you watch north, me south.
I find our zodiacs, Libra and Scorpius,
tell you the stars of Libra were once too dim
for a constellation, how Roman astrologers
removed my claws to forge your scales,
forever fusing us in the night.
The year we met, Hale-Bopp comet hung
in the sky for months like the Star of Bethlehem.
On clear nights we'd watch it from our balcony
while it burned across the wide Texas sky—
before this body of stars became an envy
with its multiplying, mine only a craving.
Last seen in the Bronze age, we imagined
those makers of Stonehenge, of Babylon,
gazing toward the same sky. Did they welcome it
with wonder or worship? I think of the 1000 years
the light takes to reach me, watch falling stars tumble
like lost children escaping the dark. You catch them all,
return my limbs, make the sky whole again.

Singing to the Gods

I can no longer decipher game trails
from dry wash scars of last year's rains.

When 14th century Peruvian graves
were found, sacrificial remains laid

with human skulls pointing west towards
the ocean to appease angry deities,

herd the seas— draw it like a blanket
over scorched terrain. Some say

we're now more civilized, but today
I tossed the body of a lifeless rabbit

into the open field like an offering,
draped dried lavender atop bison skulls

hung from thresholds. I showered water
over goldfinch gathered on acacia limbs,

hummed hymns like a benediction.
I don't know how to navigate helplessness,

which language to sing to the gods,
or how to get it all to love me back.

Left to the Sun

We watch the sparrow
weave its way

through needles
of the cholla cactus tree,

her wreathed nursery
balanced between scaffold barbs,

touched only by rays of the sun.
Each spring we decipher

wildflowers from weeds,
deciding—if it blooms, it stays.

The last to remain
are the fiddleneck and nettle

with their bristled skin,
not even chosen for a vase,

their stems lean
like lovers towards the light.

And for a moment
we don't consider the world

with all its thorned, its untouched.
We leave them to the sun.

How the Black Hole Sings

NASA released audio of how a black hole sounds.
Singing in tongues—a language of beginnings
and endings. Two seconds in, I had to turn it off.
Every emotion encapsulated into one sound lingering
in the dark, like the afterimage of a flash in the night.
The sound the room made the day my stepdaughter
invited me to witness the birth of her child,
an experience she knew I'd never have. I held her
hand and watched her face, listened to the sounds
of the room—anguish, joy, fear, and the tears when
we heard the cries of new life, combined tears
of elation for her, grief for myself. The same sounds
the room made as my father lay dying, just a few years
before—the sound of someone drowning as people
watched, helpless, from the shore. Silent sobbing
wrapped in hospiced protest when they called the hour
of his death. The same sound the room makes when we
send the dogs outside and open sliding doors to let
our joining echo across vacant hills. This is how
the black hole sings—of sex, birth and dying
and everything in between. The sound from inside
the womb, as your world contracts around you.

Even the Clothes Moth

Religion has made me afraid of dying.
With its swailing of souls, scouring
eternity for the end of forever.

And yet today, the barn owl hinges
the fencepost as a harbinger of night.
Coyotes follow, yip their apostolic battle cry.

Even the clothes moth with its 30-day-life
feasts on remnants of owl pellet fur, leaving
nothing but tiny bones of toads and voles.

And yet today, all the wounded still clamber
towards sunrise. The limbless alligator lizard
cinches its life to a crevice of creeping thistle.

All the broken in accord with every victor—

and yet today

and yet today

and yet today

Midlife

the rains have upended
the palo verde, its green
roots pushing through pavers
as though it were going
to step from the ground,
heave its grand canopy
to another life.

we too have succumbed
to its weariness, yet reined
by the sight of silkworms
carried where winds
might take them,
their gossamer webs
spun like balloons.

Burnished Ordinary

September winds cut through the mountain pass,
carve our young olive trees into wild and wiry sculptures.
Shaped by the elements, they lean with outstretched
branches as if asking to be rescued. Thankful
for being called from the monotony of the day,
we tie off small trunks, wrench in opposing directions.
We trim their pleading limbs, gently coax them upwards,
aspire to breach the sky. Now boughs heavy with harvest,
like us, their trunks stand less erect molded by time
and nature's whims. We rid the ground of pitted fruit,
fill our pails as crushed granite glistens like stardust
at our feet. Our torsos straighten, eyes rise toward canopies
swarming with golden sustenance, us wrapped
in burnished ordinary, a disco ball of dappled light.

The Color of Cocoons

Wakened again by a California towhee
charging his own reflection. He flings
himself against the glass doors, forgets
he fought this adversary the day before.

Our brains are hardwired to remember
the bad things, evolved to keep us alive,
to know where poisonous berry patches lie,
the watering hole where tigers meet.

No visceral memory of the way moonlight
reflects off velvet cattails served us,
the way flames brought shadows to life.

Tonight, the sky resembles a Turner sea,
dusk clouds, the palest cerulean blue,
underpinnings the color of cocoons,
peach as new skin—the shade of conception.

Maybe I should listen to the towhee with his
rewards in forgetting, futility of an endless fight.
Revel in the newness of a repeated sunset,
yet another wonder making it all worthwhile.

I Should Have Known

these sheets billowing on the line
would become a sail,
carry me away from this body
which now rejects every vice.
Take me to that shirtless girl
in the shelled driveway
making mudpies in rain-soaked soil.
To the font of sand and silt
collecting liquified heaven.
The patch where grass never grew,
where the earth saved a space
just for me. Cleansed of inhibitions,
alabaster skin and underwear
now the color of excavated clay.
I'm sure she never questioned
belonging, or tomorrow—or even me.
Arms and legs flapped into mud angels
in a dusk of fireflies
floating in her own bioluminescent sea.
Or how when she dried in the summer sun
she stood like a terra cotta god
taking her place among the ancients.

The Winged and the Horned

Tonight my granddaughter cried for wings,
after spending the day blowing dandelion seeds
from their stems, saying she had the same wish
for each one. *It's a secret*, she said, then whispered—
It's wings, I wished for wings.

Last night she learned fairies are born
from the laughter of children, went to bed crying,
I'm mad at God because he didn't let me have wings.

I want to tell her she should get used to being mad at God.
That we all wish we could fly—rise high enough
to nest in sequoia, where wars become plastic figures
in sandboxes, migrating easily in borderless skies.
That I once believed we all had flown until
our wings were clipped in disappointment.

Instead, I have her reach back and feel her scapula,
say, you once had wings, but now we're needed here
on the ground with the hoofed and the horned, rooted
with dandelion, where all winged things have a place to land.

Sometimes we say things we no longer believe.
I want to convince her it's all true, that children's laughter
makes the world take flight. She laughs and says,
I love them all— the winged and the horned,
my feet lifting ever so slightly from the tiled ground.

With Thanks

Thanks to my weekly Poetry Salon for helping workshop these poems over the last 4 years, Leslie Hodge, Jennifer Karp, Jen Laffler, Ron Lauderbach, Pat Obuchowski, Margaret Sullivan, Barbara Thomson, Patricia Williams and our original mentor who started this blaze, Ron Salisbury.

Thanks to Taylor Byas for her individual poetry editing.

Special thanks to Joan Kwon Glass for her manuscript editing, workshops, kind support and encouragement.

And thank-you to my loving husband, Jon Greenwood, who has always been a source of inspiration, my first reader, and my biggest advocate. To my beautiful children who have allowed me to be their mother and supported all my endeavors. And of course, my granddaughter for wishing for wings.

Thanks to all my fellow artists who continue to remind me, it's never too late.

Born in Shreveport, Louisiana, now living in Southern California, poet and printmaker, **Tammy C. Greenwood** is heavily influenced by her Southern roots and newfound connection to the West Coast. Returning to academia later in life, she graduated summa cum laude from Cal State San Bernardino earning her BA in Studio Art studying printmaking, sculpture, painting, and creative writing. She identifies as both a poet and printmaker, seamlessly moving between these two disciplines. Her connection to the natural world is apparent through her use of iconic subject matter richly woven in symbolism as she explores themes of infertility, motherhood, life, death, and immortality.

She continued her education earning a Poetry Certificate through San Diego Writer's Ink studying under San Diego poet laureate, Ron Salisbury. She is a founding member of the Poetry Salon, a weekly read and critique group which has met for the past 5 years. She is a Pushcart Prize, Best Spiritual Lit nominee and a finalist in the 2026 Mississippi Review Poetry Prize. Her work appears or is forthcoming in *Bellevue Literary Review, Greensboro Review, Mississippi Review, New Ohio Review, Rattle, Pinch, SWWIM, Whale Road Review,* and elsewhere.

She is currently an MFA student of Poetry at San Diego State University and her chapbook, "The Winged and the Horned," debuts in 2026 by Finishing Line Press. You can find more of her work at www.tammygreenwoodart.com and her Instagram @ tgreenwoodart

www.ingramcontent.com/pod-product-compliance
Lightning Source LLC
LaVergne TN
LVHW090540110826
845146LV00003B/1199

* 9 7 9 8 8 9 9 9 0 4 6 4 6 *